Copyright © 2023 by Michael Jaynes (Author)

This book is protected by copyright law and is intended solely for personal use. Reproduction, distribution, or any other form of use requires the written permission of the author. The information presented in this book is for educational and entertainment purposes only, and while every effort has been made to ensure its accuracy and completeness, no guarantees are made. The author is not providing legal, financial, medical, or professional advice, and readers should consult with a licensed professional before implementing any of the techniques discussed in this book. The content in this book has been sourced from various reliable sources, but readers should exercise their own judgment when using this information. The author is not responsible for any losses, direct or indirect, that may occur from the use of this book, including but not limited to errors, omissions, or inaccuracies.

We hope this book has been informative and helpful on your journey to understanding and celebrating older adults. Thank you for your interest and support!

Title: The Chronicles of the Enchanted Kingdom
Subtitle: A Tale of Magic and Mystery

Series: Red War Rivalries: The Evolution and Impact of Sports' Greatest Feuds
By Michael Jaynes

"Liverpool against Manchester United is probably one of the most intense rivalries in football history."
Steven Gerrard, former Liverpool captain

"The rivalry between Liverpool and Manchester United is steeped in history, and it's something that every player wants to be a part of."
Rio Ferdinand, former Manchester United defender

"It's the greatest rivalry in sports, in my opinion. When you think about the history, the passion, the intensity, it's unmatched."
Alex Rodriguez, former Yankee player

"There's just something about playing the Yankees that brings out the best in the Red Sox, and vice versa. It's a special feeling."
Dustin Pedroia, former Red Sox player

"The Celtics-Lakers rivalry is the best in all of sports."
Bill Simmons

"It's always special when the Celtics and Lakers play. The history, the tradition, the excellence of both franchises, it's all there."
Larry Bird

"The McLaren-Ferrari rivalry was so intense because they were two of the biggest and most successful teams in Formula One history. They were always pushing each other to the limit, both on and off the track."
Martin Brundle, former Formula One driver and commentator

Table of Contents

Introduction 7
The Significance of Rivalries in Sports 7
The History of Red War Competitions 9
The Psychology of Rivalries 12
The Evolution of Red War Rivalries 15
The Impact of Rivalries on Athletes and Teams 18

Chapter 1: Liverpool FC vs. Manchester United in Soccer 20
The Origins of the Rivalry 20
Key Players and Memorable Moments 22
Cultural Significance of the Derby 26
Recent Matchups and Future Prospects 29
The Impact of the Rivalry on the English Premier League 31

Chapter 2: Boston Bruins vs. Montreal Canadiens in Ice Hockey 34
Origins of the Rivalry 34
Key Players and Memorable Moments 37
Impact of the Rivalry on the NHL 39
The Importance of Playoff Series in the Rivalry 41
The Role of Enforcers in the Rivalry 44

Chapter 3: Muhammad Ali vs. Joe Frazier in Boxing 46

Origins of the Rivalry 46
Key Fights and Memorable Moments 49
Cultural Significance of the Rivalry 51
The Importance of the Thrilla in Manila 54
The Legacy of the Rivalry in Boxing History 58

Chapter 4: Ferrari vs. McLaren in Motorsports 63
Origins of the Rivalry 63
Key Drivers and Memorable Races 66
Technological Innovations and the Rivalry 71
Recent Matchups and Future Prospects 74
The Impact of the Rivalry on the Formula One World Championship 77

Conclusion 80
The Importance of Red War Rivalries 80
Lessons Learned from the Competitions 83
The Future of Red War Rivalries in Global Sports 86
The Impact of Technology on Red War Rivalries 88
The Role of Fans and Media in Fostering Rivalries 91

Key Terms and Definitions 94
Supporting Materials 96

Introduction
The Significance of Rivalries in Sports

The world of sports is filled with rivalries that inspire passion and loyalty from fans around the globe. These intense and longstanding competitions between teams and individuals, often referred to as "red wars," have played a significant role in the history and culture of sports.

One of the main reasons that rivalries are so significant in sports is that they create a heightened sense of excitement and drama for fans. When two teams or athletes with a long-standing history of competition face off against each other, it often feels like more than just a game. The stakes are higher, and the emotions are stronger. This creates an atmosphere of anticipation and tension that is unique to rivalries.

Rivalries also help to build and strengthen team identities. When a team has a rivalry with another team, it gives them a clear opponent to measure themselves against. It creates a sense of "us versus them," which can be motivating for players and fans alike. Rivalries can also help to create a sense of community and shared identity among fans, as they come together to support their team against their rivals.

In addition to these emotional and psychological benefits, rivalries can also have tangible effects on the performance of athletes and teams. Research has shown that the pressure and intensity of rivalries can have a positive impact on performance, as athletes often rise to the occasion when facing off against their rivals. This can lead to higher levels of effort and engagement, which can translate into better performance on the field or court.

However, it's important to note that not all rivalries are created equal. Some rivalries are based on longstanding traditions and histories, while others are manufactured by the media or marketing teams. The level of intensity and significance of a rivalry can vary widely depending on the context and the individuals involved.

Overall, the significance of rivalries in sports cannot be overstated. These competitions have played a significant role in the history and culture of sports, and will continue to inspire passion and loyalty from fans around the globe.

The History of Red War Competitions

The history of red war competitions is long and fascinating, stretching back to ancient times when contests of physical strength and skill were a popular form of entertainment. The earliest recorded examples of organized athletic competitions come from ancient Greece, where the Olympic Games were held every four years from 776 BC until AD 393.

While these early contests were not necessarily driven by rivalry or conflict, they set the stage for the development of more intense and competitive sporting events. Over time, rivalries began to emerge between different regions or cities, often based on a shared history of conflict or animosity. These rivalries could be found in a variety of different sports and competitions, from chariot races to gladiator fights.

As sports and games continued to evolve over the centuries, so too did the rivalries that arose between different teams or players. In medieval Europe, for example, jousting tournaments were a popular form of competition, with knights and nobles from different countries and regions vying for prestige and honor. These tournaments often became heated affairs, with rivalries between individual competitors fueling the intensity of the competition.

In the modern era, red war competitions have become a staple of professional sports, with fierce rivalries between teams and players driving interest and excitement among fans. From the fierce battles between the Boston Celtics and the Los Angeles Lakers in basketball to the historic feud between the New York Yankees and the Boston Red Sox in baseball, these rivalries have become an integral part of the sporting landscape.

One of the earliest and most famous examples of modern red war competition was the Ashes, a cricket competition between England and Australia that dates back to 1882. The rivalry between these two cricket powerhouses has since become one of the most intense and enduring in all of sports, with fans on both sides fiercely loyal to their respective teams.

Other notable examples of red war competitions include the Ryder Cup in golf, the Davis Cup in tennis, and the World Cup in soccer. In each of these competitions, national pride and the desire for victory fuel intense rivalries between teams and players from different countries and regions.

While the history of red war competitions is long and storied, it is clear that these rivalries have played a vital role in the development of sports and games throughout the ages.

As we continue to look to the future of sports, it is certain that red war competitions will continue to captivate and inspire fans around the world.

The Psychology of Rivalries

Rivalries have been a part of sports since the beginning of organized competition. These intense and passionate relationships between teams or individuals can have a significant impact on players, coaches, and fans alike. But what exactly is it about rivalries that make them so compelling? What psychological factors contribute to the creation and perpetuation of these intense relationships?

One of the main reasons that rivalries are so powerful is that they tap into our innate desire for competition and challenge. Humans have always been drawn to activities that allow us to test our skills and abilities against others, and sports provide an ideal platform for this kind of competition. Rivalries take this desire to another level by creating a highly charged and emotionally intense environment that can drive players to perform at their best.

Another psychological factor that contributes to the power of rivalries is the idea of "ingroup" and "outgroup" bias. This bias is the tendency to favor individuals who are part of our own group (ingroup) and to view individuals from other groups (outgroup) with suspicion or hostility. In sports, this bias can be magnified, as fans and players alike identify strongly with their own team and view opposing teams as rivals.

In addition, rivalries can also be driven by a sense of history and tradition. Many rivalries have their roots in longstanding cultural or regional differences, which can create a sense of pride and identity for fans and players alike. The history of past matchups and the memories associated with them can also contribute to the intensity of the rivalry.

The psychology of rivalries also extends to the impact that they can have on individual players and teams. Rivalries can create a strong sense of motivation and purpose for players, driving them to work harder and perform better than they would in other circumstances. They can also create a sense of unity and camaraderie among teammates, as they work together to defeat a common enemy.

However, rivalries can also have negative effects. The intense emotions associated with rivalries can sometimes lead to unsportsmanlike behavior, such as cheating or excessive aggression. Players may also become overly focused on the rivalry, to the detriment of their overall performance.

In conclusion, the psychology of rivalries is complex and multifaceted. These intense relationships between teams or individuals tap into our innate desire for competition and challenge, as well as our biases and sense of identity. While they can be a powerful motivator and source of pride, they can also have negative consequences if not managed appropriately. Understanding the psychology of rivalries can help players, coaches, and fans navigate these complex relationships in a healthy and productive way.

The Evolution of Red War Rivalries

Red War competitions have evolved throughout history, with rivalries becoming an integral part of their development. The term "Red War" was first coined in the early 20th century, referring to any competitive activity with a high degree of risk or danger. Over time, Red War has evolved to encompass a wide range of sports, from combat sports like boxing and MMA to team-based sports like soccer and hockey.

The evolution of Red War rivalries has been influenced by a number of factors, including changes in technology, globalization, and the media. In the early days of Red War competitions, rivalries often arose naturally between individuals or teams who competed against each other repeatedly. These rivalries were often based on personal or regional differences, and were fueled by intense emotions like pride, envy, and anger.

As Red War competitions became more organized and professionalized, the role of rivalries changed. In the mid-20th century, the rise of televised sports brought Red War competitions into homes around the world, making it easier for fans to follow their favorite athletes and teams. This increased visibility led to the growth of rivalries beyond the local level, with fans from different regions and even countries developing intense loyalties to their teams.

At the same time, advances in technology and transportation made it easier for athletes to travel and compete on a global scale. This led to the development of international Red War competitions, like the Olympics and the World Cup, which have become some of the most fiercely contested rivalries in sports history.

In recent years, the rise of social media has further fueled the evolution of Red War rivalries. Fans can now follow their favorite athletes and teams in real-time, and share their opinions and reactions with millions of others around the world. This has led to an increase in the intensity of rivalries, as fans can interact with each other directly and in real-time, creating a sense of community and shared passion around their favorite teams and athletes.

Overall, the evolution of Red War rivalries has been shaped by a complex interplay of factors, including changes in technology, globalization, and the media. While the origins of rivalries may be based on personal or regional differences, the growth of Red War competitions has transformed them into global phenomena, with fans from around the world coming together to celebrate their shared love of sports and the intense rivalries that make them so exciting.

The Impact of Rivalries on Athletes and Teams

Rivalries are an integral part of sports culture and have been a driving force behind some of the most memorable moments in sporting history. From the intense competition to the emotional highs and lows, rivalries have the power to inspire and motivate athletes and teams like nothing else.

The impact of rivalries on athletes and teams can be both positive and negative. On the one hand, rivalries can push athletes and teams to achieve new levels of excellence. The pressure of a big game or a historic rivalry can force athletes to perform at their best and push their limits. This can lead to incredible displays of skill and athleticism that fans will remember for years to come.

On the other hand, rivalries can also be a source of stress and distraction. The pressure to win can be overwhelming, and the emotional intensity of a rivalry can make it difficult for athletes to focus on the task at hand. This can lead to mistakes, poor performances, and even injuries.

In addition to the impact on individual athletes, rivalries also have a profound effect on teams as a whole. Rivalries can bring a team together, creating a sense of unity and purpose that can be difficult to achieve in any other way.

A team that is united by a common goal – to beat their rivals – can be a powerful force on the field or court.

However, rivalries can also divide a team, causing internal conflicts and distractions. The pressure to win can create tension between teammates, leading to infighting and dysfunction. This can ultimately undermine the team's performance and lead to losses on the field.

Despite the potential drawbacks, the impact of rivalries on athletes and teams is undeniable. Rivalries have the power to inspire and motivate athletes and teams to achieve greatness, and they are a key part of what makes sports so exciting and memorable for fans. As such, it is important for athletes and teams to understand the potential impact of rivalries on their performance and to find ways to use these rivalries to their advantage.

Chapter 1: Liverpool FC vs. Manchester United in Soccer

The Origins of the Rivalry

The rivalry between Liverpool FC and Manchester United is one of the oldest and most intense rivalries in football history. It all started in the late 19th century when Manchester United was known as Newton Heath and Liverpool FC was known as Everton FC and Athletic Grounds.

The first official match between the two teams was played on April 28, 1894, in a friendly match, which ended in a 2-0 victory for Liverpool FC. However, it was not until the 20th century that the rivalry began to intensify. The two teams played their first league match against each other on October 28, 1895, which ended in a 2-2 draw.

One of the earliest incidents that contributed to the rivalry was the transfer of Liverpool captain Alex Raisbeck to Manchester United in 1902. This transfer was controversial, and it led to protests from Liverpool supporters. Raisbeck's transfer was seen as a betrayal, and it fueled the animosity between the two clubs.

The rivalry between Liverpool FC and Manchester United was further intensified by their success in domestic and European competitions. Manchester United won the first of their 20 English league titles in 1908, while Liverpool FC won their first in 1901. Both teams were also successful in the FA Cup, with Manchester United winning it 12 times, and Liverpool FC winning it 7 times.

In the 1970s and 1980s, the rivalry reached new heights. During this period, Liverpool FC dominated English football, winning 11 league titles, while Manchester United struggled to keep up. However, in the late 1980s, Manchester United started to challenge Liverpool FC's dominance, winning their first league title in 26 years in 1993.

The rivalry between Liverpool FC and Manchester United is not just based on football; it is also influenced by the cultural and social differences between the two cities. Liverpool is known for its music scene and its working-class roots, while Manchester is known for its industry and its cosmopolitanism.

In conclusion, the rivalry between Liverpool FC and Manchester United is one of the oldest and most intense rivalries in football history. It started in the late 19th century and has been fueled by success in domestic and European competitions, controversial transfers, and cultural and social differences between the two cities. Despite the fierce rivalry, the two teams share a mutual respect and recognition of each other's achievements.

Key Players and Memorable Moments

The Liverpool FC vs. Manchester United rivalry has produced some of the most memorable moments and featured some of the greatest players in the history of English football. In this section, we will take a closer look at some of the key players and moments that have defined this historic rivalry.

Key Players:

1. Steven Gerrard – Liverpool

Steven Gerrard is one of the greatest players in Liverpool's history and a true legend of the game. He was a central midfielder known for his attacking prowess and his ability to score crucial goals in big games. Gerrard was a key player in Liverpool's 2005 Champions League victory and played a crucial role in many of the team's victories over Manchester United.

2. Wayne Rooney – Manchester United

Wayne Rooney is one of the most iconic players in Manchester United's history and a true legend of the game. He was a versatile forward who could play in a number of different positions and was known for his strength, pace, and ability to score goals. Rooney was a key player in many of Manchester United's victories over Liverpool, and his overhead kick goal in the 2011 Manchester derby is one of the greatest goals in Premier League history.

3. Kenny Dalglish – Liverpool

Kenny Dalglish is a true legend of Liverpool and one of the greatest players to ever play for the club. He was a forward who was known for his incredible goal-scoring ability and his clinical finishing. Dalglish was a key player in Liverpool's dominant period in the late 1970s and early 1980s, and he played a crucial role in many of the team's victories over Manchester United.

4. Ryan Giggs – Manchester United

Ryan Giggs is one of the most successful players in Manchester United's history and a true legend of the game. He was a versatile midfielder who could play in a number of different positions and was known for his incredible pace and ability to beat defenders. Giggs was a key player in many of Manchester United's victories over Liverpool, and his goal in the 1999 FA Cup semi-final replay is one of the most iconic moments in the history of the rivalry.

Memorable Moments:

1. Liverpool 3-1 Manchester United (1977)

This match is remembered as one of the greatest Liverpool victories over Manchester United. Liverpool dominated the game from start to finish, with goals from

Kevin Keegan, Jimmy Case, and Ray Kennedy. This victory helped to establish Liverpool as the dominant force in English football in the late 1970s.

2. Manchester United 2-1 Liverpool (1999)

This match is remembered for Ryan Giggs' incredible solo goal in the FA Cup semi-final replay. Giggs picked up the ball on the left wing, beat several Liverpool defenders, and smashed the ball into the roof of the net to send Manchester United to the final.

3. Liverpool 4-1 Manchester United (2009)

This match is remembered for Liverpool's dominant performance against their arch-rivals. Liverpool scored four goals in the first half, with goals from Fernando Torres, Steven Gerrard, and Andrea Dossena. This victory helped to establish Liverpool as a serious contender for the Premier League title.

4. Manchester United 1-4 Liverpool (2009)

This match is remembered as one of the greatest Liverpool victories over Manchester United. Liverpool dominated the game from start to finish, with goals from Fernando Torres, Steven Gerrard, and Andrea Dossena. This victory helped to establish Liverpool as a serious contender for the Premier League title.

Conclusion:

The Liverpool FC vs. Manchester United rivalry has produced some of the greatest players and most memorable moments in the history of English football. From Steven Gerrard and Wayne Rooney to Cristiano Ronaldo and Luis Suarez, the two clubs have seen some of the world's best talents grace their teams. Their fierce battles on the pitch have been immortalized by iconic moments, such as Gary Neville's infamous goal celebration and Steven Gerrard's slip in the 2013-14 season.

However, the rivalry extends far beyond the field of play. It has cultural, social, and economic significance, shaping the identity of the cities of Liverpool and Manchester and fueling the passions of millions of fans worldwide. The impact of this rivalry on the English Premier League is undeniable, driving competition and intensity that draws in audiences from around the world.

As we look to the future, it is clear that the Liverpool FC vs. Manchester United rivalry will continue to thrive and evolve, fueled by the passion and commitment of the players and fans alike. With new stars emerging and old ones departing, the two clubs will continue to write their story, shaping the history of English football for generations to come.

Cultural Significance of the Derby

The rivalry between Liverpool FC and Manchester United is one of the most intense in all of sports, and the cultural significance of the derby cannot be overstated. For many fans, the rivalry is about much more than just soccer – it represents a clash of identities, histories, and values.

At its core, the Liverpool-Manchester United rivalry is rooted in geography. The two cities are located just 30 miles apart, and historically they have been rivals in everything from industry to music. This rivalry has spilled over into soccer, with Liverpool and Manchester United representing the two largest and most successful cities in English soccer.

One of the most notable aspects of the Liverpool-Manchester United rivalry is the way in which it reflects broader cultural and political trends. In the 1970s and 1980s, for example, Liverpool was a city in decline, plagued by unemployment and social unrest. By contrast, Manchester was undergoing a renaissance, with investment pouring into the city and its economy booming. The rivalry between the two cities mirrored these larger societal shifts, with Liverpool representing a gritty, working-class identity and Manchester embodying a more aspirational, upwardly mobile vision of the future.

The Liverpool-Manchester United rivalry has also been shaped by historical events, particularly in the realm of soccer. The two teams have been competing against each other since the late 19th century, and their matches have produced some of the most memorable moments in English soccer history. From Eric Cantona's infamous kung-fu kick to Steven Gerrard's last-gasp goal in the 2014 match at Anfield, the Liverpool-Manchester United rivalry has provided countless moments of drama and excitement.

Another important aspect of the cultural significance of the Liverpool-Manchester United rivalry is the way in which it has been shaped by the media. British tabloids in particular have long stoked the flames of the rivalry, using sensationalist headlines and provocative stories to increase readership and generate controversy. The rivalry has also been the subject of numerous books, films, and documentaries, cementing its place in popular culture and ensuring that it will continue to be a source of fascination for years to come.

Ultimately, the cultural significance of the Liverpool-Manchester United rivalry lies in its ability to capture the imagination of fans around the world. Whether it's the passion of the supporters, the drama of the matches, or the larger societal issues that the rivalry represents, there is no denying that the Liverpool-Manchester United derby is one of the most compelling and enduring rivalries in all of sports.

Recent Matchups and Future Prospects

In recent years, the Liverpool FC vs. Manchester United rivalry has remained fiercely competitive, with both teams vying for the top spot in the Premier League. The 2019-2020 season saw Liverpool clinch their first Premier League title in 30 years, while Manchester United finished in third place, just five points behind Liverpool. The two teams faced off twice during the season, with Liverpool winning 2-0 at home in January 2020 and the teams drawing 1-1 at Old Trafford in October 2019.

The 2020-2021 season was another competitive one for the two clubs, with Manchester United finishing second in the league, just behind champions Manchester City, and Liverpool finishing in a disappointing sixth place. The two teams faced off twice during the season, with Manchester United winning 3-2 at home in January 2021 and the teams drawing 0-0 at Anfield in October 2020.

Looking ahead, the Liverpool FC vs. Manchester United rivalry shows no signs of slowing down. Both teams have invested heavily in their squads in recent years, with Liverpool adding the likes of Diogo Jota and Thiago Alcantara to their already star-studded lineup, and Manchester United bringing in Bruno Fernandes and Edinson Cavani. The rivalry between the two clubs extends beyond the pitch, with the two clubs also competing in the transfer market and off the field in terms of sponsorship and revenue.

In terms of future prospects, both Liverpool and Manchester United will be looking to add to their already impressive trophy hauls. Liverpool will be looking to regain their Premier League title and mount a serious challenge in the Champions League, while Manchester United will be aiming to go one better in the league and push for success in Europe. With both teams boasting talented squads and passionate fan bases, the Liverpool FC vs. Manchester United rivalry is sure to remain one of the most hotly contested and closely watched rivalries in world football.

The Impact of the Rivalry on the English Premier League

The rivalry between Liverpool FC and Manchester United has not only impacted the two clubs themselves but also the English Premier League as a whole. The intense competition between the two sides has raised the overall level of the league, making it more exciting and attractive to fans around the world.

In recent years, both Liverpool and Manchester United have been struggling to keep up with the other top teams in the Premier League. However, their rivalry still brings in massive audiences and generates significant revenue for the league. Their matchups are often the most watched and anticipated games of the season, with millions of fans tuning in from around the globe.

One way in which the rivalry has impacted the Premier League is through the influence of former Liverpool and Manchester United players who have gone on to become successful managers. Both Sir Alex Ferguson, former manager of Manchester United, and Jurgen Klopp, current manager of Liverpool, have had significant impacts on the league as a whole.

Ferguson's 26-year reign at Manchester United saw the club win 13 Premier League titles, five FA Cups, and two

UEFA Champions League trophies. He also developed a fierce rivalry with Liverpool during his tenure, leading his side to many famous victories over their rivals. His success at Manchester United cemented the club's position as one of the dominant forces in English football and set the standard for other teams to follow.

In contrast, Klopp's impact on Liverpool has been more recent, but no less significant. Since his arrival in 2015, Klopp has transformed Liverpool into one of the most dominant teams in Europe, winning the Premier League, Champions League, and Club World Cup. He has also reinvigorated the rivalry between Liverpool and Manchester United, with his side often getting the better of their opponents in recent years.

The impact of the Liverpool vs. Manchester United rivalry can also be seen in the transfer market, with both clubs often competing for the same players. This has led to some high-profile transfer battles, such as when Liverpool signed Virgil van Dijk from Southampton for a then-world record fee of £75 million, or when Manchester United signed Paul Pogba from Juventus for a then-world record fee of £89 million.

The rivalry between Liverpool and Manchester United is not just limited to the pitch, however. Both clubs have massive fan bases and generate significant revenue through merchandise sales, sponsorships, and other sources. The intensity of the rivalry only adds to the value of these brands, making them even more attractive to investors and sponsors.

Overall, the rivalry between Liverpool FC and Manchester United has had a profound impact on the English Premier League. It has raised the level of competition, brought in massive audiences, and influenced the league through the successes of former players turned managers. The rivalry is likely to continue for many years to come, ensuring that the Premier League remains one of the most exciting and competitive leagues in the world.

Chapter 2: Boston Bruins vs. Montreal Canadiens in Ice Hockey

Origins of the Rivalry

The Boston Bruins vs. Montreal Canadiens rivalry is one of the oldest and most intense rivalries in North American sports, dating back to the early days of the National Hockey League (NHL). The rivalry has its roots in the Original Six era of the NHL, when the league was composed of only six teams, all located in the northeastern United States and eastern Canada.

The Canadiens were founded in 1909 and are the oldest professional hockey team in the world. They were one of the founding members of the NHL in 1917, along with the Bruins. From the beginning, the Canadiens established themselves as a dominant team in the league, winning the Stanley Cup for the first time in 1916, before the formation of the NHL. Over the next few decades, the Canadiens would become the most successful franchise in NHL history, winning a total of 24 Stanley Cups.

The Bruins, on the other hand, struggled in their early years in the NHL. They did not win their first Stanley Cup until 1929, 12 years after joining the league. However, in the 1930s, the Bruins began to emerge as a strong team, led by stars such as Eddie Shore and Milt Schmidt. They won their second Stanley Cup in 1939, defeating the New York Rangers in the finals.

The rivalry between the Bruins and Canadiens began to intensify in the 1940s, as both teams became contenders for the Stanley Cup. In the 1940s and 1950s, the two teams faced each other in the playoffs numerous times, with the Canadiens usually coming out on top. However, the Bruins would finally get their revenge in 1971, when they defeated the Canadiens in the first round of the playoffs on their way to winning the Stanley Cup.

Since then, the rivalry has continued to be one of the most heated in the NHL, with both teams playing each other multiple times per season. The Bruins and Canadiens have faced each other in the playoffs 34 times, with the Canadiens winning 25 of those series. However, the Bruins have won seven of the last 11 playoff matchups between the two teams, including a memorable seven-game series in 2011 that saw the Bruins come back from a 2-0 deficit to win the series.

The origins of the Bruins vs. Canadiens rivalry are rooted in the early history of the NHL, as the two teams were two of the original six franchises. Over the years, the rivalry has grown and evolved, fueled by intense playoff battles, memorable moments, and legendary players. Today, the rivalry remains as strong as ever, with both teams still vying for supremacy in the NHL's Eastern Conference.

Key Players and Memorable Moments

The Boston Bruins and Montreal Canadiens rivalry, also known as the "Original Six" rivalry, is one of the oldest and most storied rivalries in North American sports history. Over the course of their 90-year history, the two teams have faced each other 748 times in the regular season, and another 177 times in the playoffs, with Montreal holding a slight edge in both categories.

Throughout the history of the rivalry, both teams have been blessed with some of the greatest players to ever lace up a pair of skates. From Boston, the names Bobby Orr, Phil Esposito, and Ray Bourque stand out, while from Montreal, legends like Maurice Richard, Jean Beliveau, and Guy Lafleur come to mind.

One of the most memorable moments in the rivalry occurred in 1979, during Game 7 of the Stanley Cup semifinals. The Bruins had taken a 4-3 lead late in the game on a goal by Rick Middleton, but with just 1:14 left on the clock, Montreal's Yvon Lambert scored to tie the game and send it into overtime. In the extra period, Montreal's Guy Lafleur scored the game-winning goal to send the Canadiens to the Stanley Cup Finals.

Another memorable moment occurred during the 2011 Stanley Cup Finals, when the Bruins and Canadiens faced each other for the first time in the playoffs in over 20 years. In Game 7, Boston's Nathan Horton scored the only goal of the game, lifting the Bruins to a 1-0 victory and sending them to the Stanley Cup Finals, where they would eventually win the championship.

Over the years, the Bruins and Canadiens have also had some of the fiercest on-ice battles in NHL history, with players often resorting to physical play and fights to settle their differences. Some of the most notorious brawls occurred in the 1970s and 1980s, with legendary enforcers like Boston's Terry O'Reilly and Montreal's Chris Nilan leading the charge.

Despite the heated nature of their rivalry, both teams have always had respect for each other and their shared history. In fact, the Canadiens were the first team to visit Boston's new TD Garden arena in 1995, following the demolition of the old Boston Garden.

As the two teams continue to compete against each other, new stars and new memories will undoubtedly be created, adding to the already rich history of this storied rivalry.

Impact of the Rivalry on the NHL

The rivalry between the Boston Bruins and the Montreal Canadiens has had a significant impact on the National Hockey League (NHL) over the years. The intense and often violent nature of the rivalry has drawn in fans from all over the world and has helped to establish the NHL as one of the premier professional sports leagues in North America.

One of the biggest impacts of the Bruins-Canadiens rivalry on the NHL is the increased media attention and television ratings that come with it. When these two teams face off, it's a game that many hockey fans circle on their calendars. The rivalry has been featured in countless television broadcasts, documentaries, and news stories, which has helped to generate interest in the NHL and hockey in general.

Another impact of the rivalry is the physical style of play that often accompanies these games. Both teams have historically employed tough, hard-hitting players who aren't afraid to mix it up and play a physical brand of hockey. This style of play has helped to establish the NHL as a league that values toughness and physicality, and has drawn in fans who enjoy watching the physical aspect of the game.

The Bruins-Canadiens rivalry has also had an impact on the NHL in terms of team success. Both teams have been very successful over the years, with the Canadiens holding a record 24 Stanley Cup championships and the Bruins not far behind with six championships of their own. The rivalry between these two teams has often brought out the best in each other, leading to some of the most memorable playoff series in NHL history.

Finally, the Bruins-Canadiens rivalry has had an impact on the league in terms of player development. Both teams have historically placed a strong emphasis on developing young talent and building through the draft. This has led to the development of many great players who have gone on to have successful careers in the NHL, including legends like Bobby Orr, Guy Lafleur, and Patrick Roy.

Overall, the rivalry between the Boston Bruins and the Montreal Canadiens has had a significant impact on the NHL over the years. From increased media attention and television ratings to a physical style of play and team success, this rivalry has helped to establish the NHL as one of the premier professional sports leagues in the world.

The Importance of Playoff Series in the Rivalry

Ice hockey has a long history of intense rivalries, but few are as storied as that between the Boston Bruins and the Montreal Canadiens. While the rivalry has seen countless regular season games and matchups over the years, it is the playoff series between these two teams that have truly cemented the rivalry's place in hockey history.

Since the first postseason meeting between the Bruins and the Canadiens in the 1929-1930 season, the two teams have faced off in a total of 34 playoff series, more than any other two teams in NHL history. These series have produced some of the most intense and dramatic moments in hockey history, with players on both sides elevating their game to new heights.

One of the most memorable playoff series between the two teams was the 1971 quarterfinals, in which the Canadiens eliminated the Bruins in seven games. The series is best remembered for Game 7, in which Canadiens goaltender Ken Dryden made a staggering 37 saves to secure a 4-2 victory for his team. The loss was a bitter pill for the Bruins to swallow, and it cemented the Canadiens' reputation as a team that knew how to win in the playoffs.

The two teams met in the playoffs again in 1977, in what would come to be known as the "Bloodbath" series. The series was marked by a series of brutal fights and violent incidents, including a bench-clearing brawl in Game 5. The Bruins emerged victorious in the series, but the cost was high - several players on both sides were injured, and the league was forced to take a hard look at its policies regarding violence and player safety.

Despite the occasional flashpoints of violence, the playoff series between the Bruins and Canadiens are also known for their high level of skill and intensity. In the 2008 playoffs, the two teams faced off in the first round, in a series that went the full seven games. In Game 6, the Bruins were trailing 4-2 with less than two minutes to go in the third period, but they managed to score two quick goals to send the game to overtime. In the extra frame, Bruins forward Marco Sturm scored the game-winning goal to force a Game 7. While the Bruins ultimately lost the series, the comeback in Game 6 remains one of the most memorable moments in recent playoff history.

The importance of playoff series in the Bruins-Canadiens rivalry cannot be overstated. Not only do these series bring out the best in the players on both sides, they also help to build the legend and lore of the rivalry. The playoff series between the two teams are the moments that fans remember and cherish, and they are the ones that truly cement the Bruins-Canadiens rivalry as one of the greatest in all of sports.

The Role of Enforcers in the Rivalry

Ice hockey is a physical sport, and the rivalry between the Boston Bruins and the Montreal Canadiens is no exception. Over the years, the two teams have employed players whose primary role was to protect their teammates and intimidate their opponents. These players are commonly referred to as "enforcers," and they play an important role in the Boston-Montreal rivalry.

One of the most famous enforcers in the history of the Boston-Montreal rivalry was Bruins player Terry O'Reilly. O'Reilly was known for his toughness and his willingness to stand up for his teammates. In a game in 1979, O'Reilly famously fought with the Canadiens' Doug Risebrough, and the two players continued to exchange blows even after they had been separated by the officials.

Another notable enforcer in the Boston-Montreal rivalry was Canadiens player Chris Nilan. Nilan was known for his toughness and his willingness to drop the gloves with anyone who crossed him or his teammates. In a game in 1984, Nilan famously fought with the Bruins' Jay Miller, and the two players continued to exchange blows even after they had fallen to the ice.

Enforcers like O'Reilly and Nilan played an important role in the Boston-Montreal rivalry because they helped to establish a physical presence on the ice. Their willingness to fight and to protect their teammates made the rivalry more intense and more exciting for fans.

However, the role of enforcers in ice hockey has become increasingly controversial in recent years. Some argue that fighting has no place in the sport and that enforcers should not be allowed to participate in games. Others argue that fighting is an important part of the game and that enforcers play an important role in protecting their teammates.

The NHL has taken steps to reduce fighting in the sport, and as a result, the role of enforcers in the Boston-Montreal rivalry has diminished somewhat. However, the physicality of the rivalry remains, and players on both teams continue to play with a high level of intensity and aggression.

In conclusion, the role of enforcers has played an important role in the Boston-Montreal rivalry. These players have helped to establish a physical presence on the ice and have made the rivalry more intense and exciting for fans. While the role of enforcers in ice hockey has become increasingly controversial, their impact on the Boston-Montreal rivalry cannot be denied.

Chapter 3: Muhammad Ali vs. Joe Frazier in Boxing
Origins of the Rivalry

Muhammad Ali and Joe Frazier were two of the greatest heavyweight boxers of all time, and their rivalry is one of the most famous in the history of sports. The origins of their rivalry can be traced back to their early careers, as both men were rising stars in the sport in the 1960s.

Ali, then known as Cassius Clay, won the Olympic gold medal in 1960 and turned professional soon after. He quickly became known for his brash personality and his ability to back up his talk in the ring. Frazier, on the other hand, grew up in poverty in South Carolina and began boxing as a way to escape his circumstances. He won the Olympic gold medal in 1964 and turned professional soon after.

Ali and Frazier's paths first crossed in 1967, when Ali was stripped of his heavyweight title for refusing to be drafted into the U.S. military during the Vietnam War. Frazier won the vacant title by defeating Buster Mathis in a 12-round decision.

Ali returned to the ring in 1970 after a three-year absence, and he immediately set his sights on Frazier and his title. The two men agreed to fight in what was billed as the

"Fight of the Century" on March 8, 1971, at Madison Square Garden in New York City.

The buildup to the fight was intense, with Ali taunting Frazier in the media and calling him an Uncle Tom. Frazier was furious, and he vowed to teach Ali a lesson in the ring. The fight itself lived up to the hype, with both men trading blows in a brutal battle that went the distance. In the end, Frazier emerged as the victor, winning by unanimous decision.

The rivalry between Ali and Frazier continued for years, with the two men fighting twice more in their careers. Ali won a 12-round decision in their second fight in 1974, but Frazier got his revenge in their third and final fight in 1975, winning by TKO in the 14th round.

The rivalry between Ali and Frazier was about more than just boxing. It was a clash of personalities and values, with Ali representing the anti-establishment counterculture of the 1960s and Frazier representing the traditional values of hard work and determination. Their fights were about more than just titles and money; they were about pride, honor, and respect.

In conclusion, the rivalry between Muhammad Ali and Joe Frazier was born out of their early careers as rising stars in the sport of boxing. Their first fight, the "Fight of the

Century," was one of the most hyped and intense in boxing history, and their subsequent fights only added to the drama and intrigue. But their rivalry was about more than just boxing; it was a clash of personalities and values that captivated the world and left an indelible mark on the sport.

Key Fights and Memorable Moments

The rivalry between Muhammad Ali and Joe Frazier is known for some of the greatest fights in boxing history, each with their own memorable moments. Here are some of the key fights and moments that defined their rivalry:

1. Fight of the Century - March 8, 1971: The first fight between Ali and Frazier, billed as the "Fight of the Century," was held at Madison Square Garden in New York City. It was the first time two undefeated heavyweight champions faced off in the ring. The fight went the full 15 rounds, with Frazier winning by unanimous decision. The most memorable moment of the fight was in the 15th round, when Frazier landed a left hook that knocked Ali down for the first time in his career.

2. Super Fight II - January 28, 1974: The second fight between Ali and Frazier, known as "Super Fight II," took place in New York City. Ali won the fight by unanimous decision after 12 rounds, but the most memorable moment was a vicious left hook from Ali that knocked Frazier down in the second round.

3. Thrilla in Manila - October 1, 1975: The third and final fight between Ali and Frazier, known as the "Thrilla in Manila," was held in the Philippines. The fight was brutal, with both fighters taking heavy damage. The most

memorable moment of the fight came in the 14th round, when Frazier's trainer, Eddie Futch, stopped the fight to save Frazier from further punishment. The fight is considered one of the greatest in boxing history.

4. The War of Words: Ali and Frazier's rivalry was not limited to the ring. They engaged in a war of words outside of the ring, with Ali often mocking Frazier's appearance and calling him a "gorilla." Frazier, in turn, resented Ali's arrogance and boasted about his own accomplishments in the ring.

5. The Fight for the Heavyweight Crown: Ali and Frazier's rivalry was not just a personal one, but also a battle for the heavyweight crown. Their fights were seen as battles between two of the greatest heavyweight champions of all time, with the winner being considered the best in the world.

Overall, the fights between Ali and Frazier were some of the most exciting and memorable in boxing history. Their rivalry extended beyond the ring and captivated the world, making them two of the most iconic figures in the sport.

Cultural Significance of the Rivalry

The rivalry between Muhammad Ali and Joe Frazier in boxing was not just significant for the sport, but also for its cultural impact on American society. The two boxers represented more than just their individual fighting styles and personalities, but also larger societal issues.

One of the key factors that made the rivalry between Ali and Frazier culturally significant was the political and social climate of the time. The 1960s and 70s were marked by significant social and political upheavals, including the Civil Rights Movement, the Vietnam War, and the Women's Liberation Movement. Ali, who had converted to Islam and changed his name from Cassius Clay, became a vocal opponent of the Vietnam War and refused to be drafted into the military. His activism and outspokenness on political issues made him a polarizing figure in American society, especially among conservatives.

On the other hand, Frazier was seen as a more traditional figure, embodying the hardworking and blue-collar ethos of the time. He was known for his toughness and perseverance, qualities that were highly valued in the working-class communities where he grew up. Frazier was also a symbol of African American success in the face of adversity, having grown up in poverty in South Carolina before becoming a world champion boxer.

The first fight between Ali and Frazier, which took place in 1971, was billed as the "Fight of the Century" and captured the attention of the entire country. It was not just a battle between two boxers, but also a clash of ideologies and values. Ali represented the anti-war and anti-establishment sentiments of the time, while Frazier represented the more traditional values of hard work, perseverance, and patriotism.

The fight itself was a grueling 15-round battle that saw both boxers push themselves to their limits. Frazier ultimately emerged victorious, dealing Ali his first professional loss. The rematch, dubbed the "Super Fight" was held in 1974, and once again, it captured the attention of the nation. Ali emerged victorious in this fight, and the two boxers would go on to face each other in a third fight, the "Thrilla in Manila," which is widely regarded as one of the greatest fights in boxing history.

Beyond the boxing ring, the rivalry between Ali and Frazier had a significant impact on American culture. It reflected the larger societal tensions and divisions of the time, particularly around issues of race, class, and political ideology. Ali's vocal opposition to the Vietnam War and his embrace of Islam made him a polarizing figure in American society, while Frazier's hardworking and patriotic image appealed to a different segment of the population. The rivalry between these two boxers, and the larger cultural forces they represented, helped to shape the cultural landscape of the time.

In conclusion, the rivalry between Muhammad Ali and Joe Frazier in boxing was not just significant for the sport, but also for its impact on American culture. The two boxers represented different values and ideologies that reflected larger societal tensions and divisions. The "Fight of the Century" and the subsequent rematches captured the attention of the entire country, and the impact of their rivalry extended far beyond the boxing ring.

The Importance of the Thrilla in Manila

The Thrilla in Manila was the third and final fight in the Muhammad Ali vs. Joe Frazier rivalry, and it remains one of the most important fights in boxing history. The fight took place on October 1, 1975, in Manila, Philippines, and it was the culmination of years of intense rivalry and bad blood between Ali and Frazier. In this section, we will explore the significance of the Thrilla in Manila and its impact on boxing and the wider culture.

The Background

Before we delve into the importance of the Thrilla in Manila, it's important to understand the context in which the fight took place. Ali and Frazier had already fought twice before, with each fighter winning one fight. Their first fight, which took place in 1971, was billed as the "Fight of the Century," and it lived up to the hype. Frazier won a unanimous decision in a brutal 15-round battle that left both fighters battered and bloodied. The second fight, which took place in 1974, was not as closely contested, with Ali winning by TKO in the 12th round.

The buildup to the third fight was marked by intense animosity between the two fighters. Ali had mocked Frazier mercilessly in the lead-up to their first fight, calling him an "Uncle Tom" and a "gorilla." Frazier, in turn, saw Ali as a loudmouthed braggart who disrespected the sport of boxing. The two men genuinely despised each other, and their rivalry was one of the most bitter and intense in the history of sports.

The Fight

The Thrilla in Manila was a grueling, brutal affair that lasted 14 rounds. Both fighters landed heavy blows throughout the fight, and both were badly hurt at different points. In the end, it was Ali who emerged victorious, as Frazier's trainer threw in the towel before the start of the 15th round.

The fight is notable for its intensity and the incredible physical toll it took on both fighters. Ali later called it the closest thing to dying that he had ever experienced, while Frazier said that he had never been in so much pain in his life. The fight is widely regarded as one of the greatest in boxing history, and it remains a defining moment in the careers of both Ali and Frazier.

The Significance

The Thrilla in Manila was significant for a number of reasons. First and foremost, it was the culmination of one of the greatest rivalries in sports history. Ali and Frazier were bitter enemies who genuinely despised each other, and their three fights were among the most memorable in boxing history. The Thrilla in Manila, in particular, was a fitting end to their rivalry, as it was a brutal, exhausting, and thrilling battle that left both fighters battered and bloodied.

The fight was also significant for its impact on boxing and the wider culture. The Thrilla in Manila was watched by an estimated one billion people worldwide, and it remains one of the most-watched fights in history. The fight was a cultural phenomenon, and it helped to cement boxing's place as one of the most popular sports in the world.

The Thrilla in Manila was also significant for its impact on Ali and Frazier's legacies. For Ali, the fight was a triumph of skill, endurance, and sheer willpower. He proved that he was still one of the best fighters in the world, even after years of inactivity and a debilitating illness. For Frazier, the fight was a heartbreaking defeat that marked the end of his career as a top-level fighter. Frazier would go on to fight a few more times, but he was never the same after the Thrilla in Manila.

*****

In addition to its impact on Ali and Frazier's legacies, the Thrilla in Manila also had broader significance for the sport of boxing. The fight is widely regarded as one of the greatest boxing matches of all time, and it helped to cement the Ali-Frazier rivalry as one of the greatest in the history of the sport. The intense animosity and competitive spirit between the two fighters, combined with their remarkable skills and courage, made for an unforgettable spectacle that captivated the world.

The Thrilla in Manila also marked the end of an era in boxing. It was the last of the three legendary fights between Ali and Frazier, and it came at a time when the sport was undergoing significant changes. The rise of new stars like Sugar Ray Leonard and Thomas Hearns, along with the emergence of new weight classes and the proliferation of championship belts, signaled a shift away from the old guard of heavyweight boxing.

Nevertheless, the Thrilla in Manila remains a touchstone for boxing fans and historians alike. It embodies the essence of what makes boxing such a compelling and enduring sport: the courage and determination of its fighters, the drama and excitement of its biggest bouts, and the larger-than-life personalities that capture our imaginations and inspire us to greatness. For Ali and Frazier, the Thrilla in Manila was the ultimate test of their will, skill, and character. For boxing fans, it remains a testament to the sport's enduring appeal and its ability to unite and inspire people across generations and cultures.

The Legacy of the Rivalry in Boxing History

The rivalry between Muhammad Ali and Joe Frazier was one of the most intense and enduring in the history of boxing. The two fighters faced each other three times in the ring, each bout becoming a cultural event that captured the attention of the world. But their rivalry was about more than just boxing; it was a clash of personalities, styles, and political ideologies. And even today, more than 50 years after their first fight, the legacy of Ali and Frazier's rivalry continues to resonate in the sport of boxing.

Ali and Frazier first fought in 1971 in what was dubbed the "Fight of the Century." Ali was coming back to boxing after being stripped of his title and banned from the sport for three years for refusing to be drafted into the Vietnam War. Frazier was the reigning heavyweight champion and had a perfect record of 26-0. The buildup to the fight was intense, with both fighters engaging in a war of words that added to the drama and excitement.

The fight itself lived up to the hype, with Frazier winning a unanimous decision in a grueling 15-round battle. But the fight was more than just a sporting event; it was a cultural moment that reflected the political and social divisions of the time. Ali was seen as a symbol of the anti-war and civil rights movements, while Frazier was seen as a representative of the establishment and the status quo. The fight was seen as a battle between two different visions of America, and the outcome was interpreted in different ways depending on one's political and social beliefs.

Their second fight, dubbed the "Super Fight II," took place in 1974 in Madison Square Garden. Ali won a unanimous decision in a less thrilling bout, but it was the third fight that cemented their rivalry in the annals of boxing history. The Thrilla in Manila, as it was called, took place in 1975 in the Philippines and was a brutal, back-and-forth battle that lasted 14 rounds. Ali ultimately emerged victorious when Frazier's trainer, Eddie Futch, threw in the towel before the final round. The fight was one of the greatest in boxing history and was seen as a testament to the bravery and skill of both fighters.

The legacy of Ali and Frazier's rivalry is felt in many ways in the sport of boxing. Their three fights are often cited as examples of the greatest matches in boxing history, and their rivalry is seen as a model for the kind of intense, personal, and meaningful rivalries that can elevate the sport. The two fighters also represented different styles of boxing, with Ali's quick footwork and lightning-fast punches contrasting with Frazier's brute strength and relentless pressure. Their fights were seen as clashes of styles and approaches, and their rivalry helped to showcase the diversity of the sport.

But perhaps the most enduring legacy of Ali and Frazier's rivalry is the way it transcended boxing and became a cultural touchstone. Their fights were seen as emblematic of larger societal issues, such as race, politics, and identity. Ali's status as a cultural icon and political activist added to the significance of their rivalry, as did Frazier's representation of a more traditional, establishment vision of America. The way in which their rivalry was framed and interpreted reflected the larger cultural debates of the time and showed how boxing could be a forum for discussing and working through important social issues.

*****

Ali and Frazier's rivalry was emblematic of the larger societal issues of the time, especially in the United States. Ali was a prominent figure in the Civil Rights Movement and was known for his vocal opposition to the Vietnam War. He was stripped of his boxing titles and banned from the sport for three years for refusing to be drafted, but he remained a symbol of resistance and defiance for many. Frazier, on the other hand, was seen as more representative of traditional American values and the establishment.

Their contrasting personalities and political beliefs were often highlighted in the media, and their fights were framed as more than just athletic contests. For example, the "Fight of the Century" was billed as a battle between "the Black Muslim versus the Great White Hope." Ali was seen as representing the Black Power movement, while Frazier was seen as embodying a more conservative, "All-American" ideal.

The rivalry between Ali and Frazier also highlighted the ways in which boxing could be a forum for discussing and working through important social issues. In many ways, boxing served as a microcosm of larger societal debates, and the fighters themselves were seen as symbols of different values and ideologies.

The legacy of Ali and Frazier's rivalry can be seen in the way that boxing has continued to be a platform for discussing and addressing social issues. For example, in recent years, athletes like Colin Kaepernick have used their platform to protest police brutality and racial injustice. The tradition of athletes speaking out on social and political issues can be traced back to the example set by Ali, who was willing to risk everything for his beliefs.

Moreover, Ali and Frazier's rivalry set a new standard for the level of passion and intensity that could be brought to the sport of boxing. Their fights were seen as epic battles between two titans, and their rivalry remains a touchstone for generations of boxing fans. The fact that their fights are still being analyzed and discussed today speaks to the lasting impact of their rivalry on the sport of boxing and on popular culture more broadly.

In conclusion, the rivalry between Muhammad Ali and Joe Frazier was one of the most intense and culturally significant rivalries in the history of sports. Their contrasting personalities and political beliefs, as well as their athletic prowess, made their fights not just athletic contests, but also cultural touchstones that reflected larger societal issues. The legacy of their rivalry can be seen in the way that boxing has continued to be a platform for discussing and addressing social issues, as well as in the lasting impact that their fights have had on popular culture.

Chapter 4: Ferrari vs. McLaren in Motorsports
Origins of the Rivalry

The rivalry between Ferrari and McLaren in motorsports has deep roots, dating back to the early days of Formula One racing. Both teams have a rich history and a long list of accomplishments, but their rivalry has been shaped by a number of key factors.

One of the main origins of the Ferrari vs. McLaren rivalry can be traced back to the 1960s, when both teams emerged as dominant forces in Formula One. Ferrari was founded in 1947 by Enzo Ferrari, who was passionate about racing and had a deep understanding of engineering and design. The team quickly became one of the most successful in the sport, winning its first championship in 1952.

McLaren, on the other hand, was founded in 1963 by Bruce McLaren, a former driver for the Cooper team. The team quickly established itself as a competitive force in Formula One, thanks to its innovative designs and engineering expertise. In 1968, the team won its first championship, with driver Denny Hulme behind the wheel.

Despite their different origins, Ferrari and McLaren quickly became fierce rivals on the track. Their battles were marked by close racing, technical innovation, and the pursuit of excellence. As the 1960s gave way to the 1970s, their rivalry only intensified, with both teams pushing the limits of what was possible in terms of design and performance.

Another factor that contributed to the rivalry was the personalities involved. Enzo Ferrari was known for his fierce competitiveness and his uncompromising approach to racing. He was deeply involved in the day-to-day operations of the team and demanded nothing less than perfection from his drivers and engineers. Bruce McLaren, on the other hand, was known for his technical expertise and his ability to push the limits of what was possible in terms of design and engineering. He was deeply respected in the racing community for his innovative ideas and his commitment to excellence.

The rivalry between Ferrari and McLaren was also shaped by the larger context of Formula One racing. Throughout the 1960s and 1970s, the sport was going through a period of rapid change, with new technologies and designs pushing the limits of what was possible on the track. Both Ferrari and McLaren were at the forefront of these changes, constantly pushing each other to be better and faster.

In conclusion, the origins of the Ferrari vs. McLaren rivalry can be traced back to the 1960s, when both teams emerged as dominant forces in Formula One racing. Their battles were marked by close racing, technical innovation, and the pursuit of excellence. The personalities involved, the larger context of Formula One racing, and their shared passion for the sport all contributed to the intensity of their rivalry.

Key Drivers and Memorable Races

The rivalry between Ferrari and McLaren has produced some of the most iconic moments in motorsports history. The teams have been involved in countless battles on the track, and their drivers have pushed each other to the limit. In this section, we will explore some of the key drivers and memorable races that have defined the Ferrari-McLaren rivalry.

1. Niki Lauda vs. James Hunt One of the most famous rivalries in Formula One history was the battle between Niki Lauda and James Hunt. Lauda was the reigning champion when Hunt joined the McLaren team in 1976, and the two drivers quickly became bitter rivals. The season culminated in a thrilling finale at the Japanese Grand Prix, where Lauda famously withdrew from the race due to unsafe track conditions. Hunt won the race and the championship, but Lauda's courage and determination in returning to racing after a horrific accident earlier in the season earned him the respect of fans around the world.

2. Ayrton Senna vs. Alain Prost The rivalry between Ayrton Senna and Alain Prost is another legendary battle in Formula One history. The two drivers were teammates at McLaren in 1988 and 1989, but their relationship quickly soured as they fought for the championship. The defining

moment of their rivalry came at the 1989 Japanese Grand Prix, where Senna controversially collided with Prost on the first lap of the race, taking them both out of the race and securing the championship for Senna.

3. Michael Schumacher vs. Mika Hakkinen The rivalry between Michael Schumacher and Mika Hakkinen in the late 1990s and early 2000s was one of the most intense in Formula One history. Schumacher dominated the sport with Ferrari, winning five consecutive championships from 2000 to 2004, but he was pushed to his limits by Hakkinen, who won back-to-back championships for McLaren in 1998 and 1999. The two drivers engaged in many thrilling battles on the track, including the famous "passing under yellow" incident at the 1998 Belgian Grand Prix.

4. Fernando Alonso vs. Lewis Hamilton In the late 2000s, the rivalry between Fernando Alonso and Lewis Hamilton brought renewed excitement to the sport. Alonso had won back-to-back championships with Renault in 2005 and 2006, but he was unable to repeat that success when he moved to McLaren in 2007. Hamilton, a rookie driver, burst onto the scene and quickly established himself as a serious contender, leading to tension between the two drivers. The season culminated in a dramatic finale at the Brazilian

Grand Prix, where Hamilton narrowly edged out Alonso and Ferrari's Kimi Raikkonen to win the championship.

5. Sebastian Vettel vs. Jenson Button The rivalry between Sebastian Vettel and Jenson Button in the early 2010s was characterized by their contrasting styles of driving. Vettel was known for his aggressive, attacking style, while Button was more strategic and measured. The two drivers engaged in many thrilling battles on the track, including the famous "Multi 21" incident at the 2013 Malaysian Grand Prix, where Vettel ignored team orders and overtook his teammate Mark Webber to win the race.

Overall, the Ferrari-McLaren rivalry has produced some of the most exciting moments in motorsports history, thanks in large part to the talented drivers who have competed for these iconic teams. Whether it's Lauda vs. Hunt, Senna vs. Prost, Schumacher vs. Hakkinen, Alonso vs. Hamilton, or Vettel vs. Button, the battles between Ferrari and McLaren drivers have captivated fans around the world and left an indelible mark on the sport. Here are some of the most memorable races in the history of the Ferrari-McLaren rivalry:

1. 1976 Japanese Grand Prix - This race is widely regarded as one of the greatest in Formula One history. Ferrari's Niki Lauda and McLaren's James Hunt were neck-

and-neck in the championship standings, and the race at Fuji Speedway would determine the title. In treacherous conditions, Lauda decided to retire from the race, giving Hunt the lead he needed to secure the championship.

2. 1988 Italian Grand Prix - This race was dominated by McLaren's Ayrton Senna, who took pole position and led from start to finish. Ferrari's Gerhard Berger finished in second place, but was over 50 seconds behind Senna at the end of the race. This was a pivotal moment in the championship, as Senna went on to win the title that year.

3. 2000 Austrian Grand Prix - This race was marred by controversy, as Ferrari's Rubens Barrichello was ordered to move over and let teammate Michael Schumacher win the race. The move was widely criticized and led to a change in the rules regarding team orders. The incident also added fuel to the fire of the already heated Ferrari-McLaren rivalry.

4. 2007 European Grand Prix - This race saw McLaren's Fernando Alonso and Lewis Hamilton battling for the lead, while Ferrari's Kimi Raikkonen was making his way through the field. In the end, Raikkonen emerged victorious, with Alonso and Hamilton finishing in second and third, respectively. The race was a turning point in the championship, as Raikkonen went on to win the title that year.

5. 2010 Canadian Grand Prix - This race was a thriller, with McLaren's Jenson Button and Ferrari's Fernando Alonso battling for the lead in the closing stages. In the end, it was Button who emerged victorious, overtaking Alonso on the final lap to take the win. The race showcased the talents of both drivers and added another chapter to the storied Ferrari-McLaren rivalry.

Technological Innovations and the Rivalry

The Ferrari-McLaren rivalry has not only been characterized by the intense competition between drivers but also by the technological innovations developed by the two teams. Both Ferrari and McLaren have a long history of pushing the boundaries of engineering and design in motorsports, and their rivalry has spurred on some of the most significant technological advancements in the sport's history.

One of the most significant innovations that emerged from the Ferrari-McLaren rivalry was the development of the semi-automatic gearbox. In the mid-1980s, Ferrari introduced the first semi-automatic gearbox in Formula One racing, which was a major breakthrough in motorsports technology. The semi-automatic gearbox allowed drivers to shift gears without using a clutch pedal, making gear changes quicker and more precise. This technology gave Ferrari a competitive edge over its rivals, and other teams soon followed suit, with McLaren introducing its own version of the semi-automatic gearbox shortly thereafter.

Another important innovation that emerged from the Ferrari-McLaren rivalry was the use of carbon fiber in Formula One cars. In the early 1980s, McLaren was the first team to introduce a carbon fiber monocoque chassis in a

Formula One car. This technology was a significant breakthrough in motorsports, as carbon fiber is lighter and stronger than the traditional materials used in car construction. The use of carbon fiber allowed McLaren to develop a lighter and more aerodynamic car, which gave the team a significant advantage over its rivals.

Ferrari was quick to adopt carbon fiber technology and soon began to incorporate it into its own cars. However, the rivalry between the two teams continued to drive innovation, and they continued to develop new and innovative ways to use carbon fiber in their cars. Today, carbon fiber is a standard material in Formula One car construction, and its use has revolutionized the sport.

The Ferrari-McLaren rivalry also played a role in the development of electronic driver aids. In the early 1990s, both teams began to use electronic systems to improve the performance of their cars. Ferrari was the first team to introduce traction control, which helped drivers to maintain control of their cars in difficult conditions. McLaren soon followed suit, introducing its own version of traction control.

The use of electronic driver aids became a contentious issue in motorsports, with some arguing that they made the sport less challenging and exciting. However, the use of these technologies continued to grow, and they are now a standard part of Formula One racing.

In addition to these technological advancements, the rivalry between Ferrari and McLaren also led to improvements in engine technology. Both teams invested heavily in the development of more powerful and efficient engines, and their innovations have had a lasting impact on motorsports. Ferrari introduced the first turbocharged engine in Formula One racing, which was a significant breakthrough in engine design. McLaren also made significant advances in engine technology, developing some of the most powerful engines in Formula One history.

Overall, the Ferrari-McLaren rivalry has been characterized by an intense competition that has driven innovation and technological advancements in motorsports. The two teams have pushed the boundaries of engineering and design, and their rivalry has played a significant role in the evolution of Formula One racing. Today, both teams continue to be at the forefront of technological innovation, and their rivalry remains one of the most compelling stories in motorsports.

Recent Matchups and Future Prospects

The Ferrari-McLaren rivalry has continued into the 21st century, with both teams still competing at the highest levels of motorsports. In recent years, the rivalry has shifted somewhat, with Mercedes emerging as the dominant team in Formula One. However, Ferrari and McLaren remain formidable opponents, and their battles on the track continue to captivate fans around the world.

Recent Matchups

In recent years, Ferrari and McLaren have continued to compete against each other in Formula One, with varying degrees of success. Ferrari has had some strong seasons, including a second-place finish in the 2018 constructors' championship, while McLaren has struggled at times, finishing sixth in the same year.

One of the most memorable recent matchups between the two teams came in the 2010 season, when Ferrari's Fernando Alonso and McLaren's Lewis Hamilton battled for the drivers' championship. The two drivers traded blows throughout the season, with Hamilton ultimately coming out on top by just four points. The rivalry between Alonso and Hamilton was intense, with both drivers pushing each other to their limits on the track.

Another recent matchup between Ferrari and McLaren came in the 2012 season, when the teams battled for the podium in the Brazilian Grand Prix. Ferrari's Fernando Alonso and McLaren's Jenson Button both finished on the podium, with Button taking the victory and Alonso finishing in third place. The race was a thrilling back-and-forth battle between the two teams, with both drivers showing off their skills and pushing their cars to the limit.

Future Prospects

Looking ahead, the future of the Ferrari-McLaren rivalry is uncertain. While both teams remain competitive, they face stiff competition from other teams, particularly Mercedes. However, both Ferrari and McLaren have strong driver lineups and are known for their ability to innovate and adapt.

One factor that could play a role in the future of the rivalry is the ongoing debate over the use of hybrid engines in Formula One. Ferrari has traditionally been a proponent of hybrid technology, while McLaren has been more skeptical. As the sport continues to evolve, it will be interesting to see how these two teams approach the use of new technologies and whether their differing perspectives will lead to renewed tensions on the track.

Another factor to consider is the potential for new teams to emerge and challenge the dominance of established teams like Ferrari and McLaren. While this is always a possibility in motorsports, the high cost of entry and the complexity of building a competitive Formula One team make it unlikely that any new teams will emerge in the near future.

Despite these uncertainties, one thing is certain: the Ferrari-McLaren rivalry has left an indelible mark on the world of motorsports. From the early battles between Enzo Ferrari and Bruce McLaren to the recent matchups between Fernando Alonso and Lewis Hamilton, these two iconic teams have pushed each other to new heights and provided fans with some of the most thrilling moments in the history of Formula One. As long as these two teams continue to compete, the rivalry between Ferrari and McLaren will remain a defining feature of the sport.

The Impact of the Rivalry on the Formula One World Championship

The rivalry between Ferrari and McLaren has had a significant impact on the world of Formula One, both in terms of the sport's popularity and its technological development. In this section, we will explore the ways in which the rivalry has shaped the Formula One World Championship and how it has influenced the sport's evolution over the years.

One of the most obvious impacts of the Ferrari-McLaren rivalry on the Formula One World Championship is the increased interest and attention it has generated from fans and media alike. The battles between these two legendary teams have provided some of the most exciting and memorable moments in motorsports history, and their duels on the track have been watched by millions of fans around the world. The rivalry has helped to raise the profile of Formula One and has contributed to the sport's growing popularity in recent years.

But the impact of the Ferrari-McLaren rivalry extends far beyond mere spectatorship. The technological innovations and advancements that have been spurred on by this rivalry have played a significant role in shaping the Formula One World Championship. Both Ferrari and

McLaren have been at the forefront of technological development in motorsports, constantly pushing the boundaries of what is possible and exploring new ways to gain a competitive edge on the track.

Perhaps the most notable technological innovation to emerge from the Ferrari-McLaren rivalry is the use of carbon fiber materials in Formula One cars. McLaren was the first team to introduce carbon fiber technology to Formula One, and Ferrari quickly followed suit. Carbon fiber materials offer significant advantages in terms of strength, rigidity, and weight, making them ideal for use in high-performance racing cars. Today, carbon fiber is a standard material used in almost all Formula One cars, and it is widely regarded as one of the most important technological advancements in the history of the sport.

Another area in which the Ferrari-McLaren rivalry has had a significant impact on the Formula One World Championship is in the development of aerodynamic technologies. Both teams have invested heavily in research and development of aerodynamic systems, with the goal of improving the performance and speed of their cars. This has led to the creation of advanced aerodynamic packages that utilize complex wind tunnels, computational fluid dynamics, and other advanced technologies to optimize the airflow around the car and reduce drag.

The rivalry has also played a role in the evolution of safety standards in Formula One. In the wake of several high-profile accidents in the late 1990s and early 2000s, both Ferrari and McLaren were instrumental in pushing for improved safety measures, such as the introduction of stronger and more durable chassis, improved crash testing protocols, and the development of more effective driver safety equipment.

In recent years, the Ferrari-McLaren rivalry has continued to shape the Formula One World Championship, even as new teams and drivers have emerged to challenge their dominance. Both teams remain at the forefront of technological innovation and development, and they continue to push the boundaries of what is possible in motorsports. As the sport continues to evolve and new challenges emerge, it is likely that the rivalry between Ferrari and McLaren will remain a driving force in the Formula One World Championship for years to come.

Conclusion
The Importance of Red War Rivalries

Red war rivalries have played an important role in the history of sports, and their significance extends far beyond the playing field. These rivalries have captured the imagination of fans and become cultural touchstones that reflect larger societal issues. They have also spurred technological innovation and shaped the evolution of sports themselves.

One of the key reasons why red war rivalries are so important is their ability to inspire passion and loyalty among fans. When two teams or athletes are locked in a heated rivalry, it creates a sense of intensity and excitement that draws people in. Fans become deeply invested in the outcome of each matchup, and the anticipation leading up to these contests can be palpable. This level of engagement helps to build a sense of community among fans, and it reinforces the idea that sports are more than just games - they are social events that bring people together.

But the impact of red war rivalries extends far beyond the fan base. These rivalries have the ability to shape cultural narratives and reflect larger societal issues. For example, the rivalry between Ali and Frazier was not just about two boxers competing for a championship - it was also a reflection of the larger cultural debates of the time, such as race, politics, and identity. Similarly, the Ferrari-McLaren rivalry has been seen as a battle between different visions of motorsports, with Ferrari representing tradition and McLaren representing innovation. The way these rivalries are framed and interpreted reflects the larger cultural forces at play in society.

In addition to their cultural significance, red war rivalries have also spurred technological innovation and shaped the evolution of sports themselves. The arms race between Ferrari and McLaren led to the development of groundbreaking technologies, such as active suspension, aerodynamic advancements, and electronic driver aids. These innovations not only gave the competing teams an edge on the track, but they also helped to advance the sport as a whole.

Furthermore, red war rivalries have a lasting impact on the sports in which they occur. They shape the narratives of those sports and help to define their histories. The legacies of Ali and Frazier, the battles between the Boston Bruins and the Montreal Canadiens, and the fierce competition between Ferrari and McLaren have all left an indelible mark on the sports in which they took place. They have become part of the lore of those sports and are retold by fans and historians for generations to come.

In conclusion, red war rivalries are an essential part of the sports landscape. They inspire passion and loyalty among fans, reflect larger cultural narratives, spur technological innovation, and shape the evolution of sports themselves. Whether it's boxing, ice hockey, or motorsports, these rivalries have become cultural touchstones that endure long after the last game or race has been run. They remind us of the power of sports to bring people together and to reflect the larger forces at play in society.

Lessons Learned from the Competitions

Throughout this book, we have explored some of the most iconic and enduring rivalries in sports history, from the Red Sox vs. Yankees in baseball to the Ferrari vs. McLaren in motorsports. While each of these rivalries is unique in its own way, they all share certain commonalities that make them particularly fascinating and important.

One of the key lessons we can learn from these rivalries is the importance of competition in driving excellence and innovation. In each of these cases, the competition between two teams or individuals spurred them to push the limits of what was possible in their sport. Whether it was through technological innovations, strategic adjustments, or simply sheer determination, these rivalries helped to raise the bar for everyone involved and set new standards of excellence.

Another important lesson from these rivalries is the role that they can play in shaping the larger cultural and historical narratives. In many cases, the battles between these teams or individuals were seen as emblematic of larger social, political, or economic tensions. They became symbols of larger struggles, and the outcomes of these competitions were often interpreted as victories or defeats for one side or the other. This is particularly true of the Red War rivalries, which were often framed in terms of national identity and geopolitical power.

But perhaps the most important lesson we can learn from these rivalries is the power of passion and fandom in sports. Whether you are a die-hard fan of the Red Sox or the Yankees, Ferrari or McLaren, or any other team or individual, the passion and energy that you bring to your support can be a source of tremendous joy and inspiration. It can bring people together across all kinds of divides and create a sense of community and shared purpose that is truly special.

Of course, it is important to remember that sports rivalries are ultimately just games, and that there are more important things in life than winning or losing. But at their best, these rivalries can be sources of inspiration, excitement, and even transcendence. They can remind us of the power of human creativity, drive, and perseverance, and they can help us to connect with something larger than ourselves.

In conclusion, the rivalries we have explored in this book are more than just games or competitions. They are stories of passion, determination, and excellence that have captured the imaginations of millions of people around the world. By understanding and appreciating these rivalries, we can learn valuable lessons about competition, culture, and human nature, and we can connect with the timeless beauty and power of sports.

The Future of Red War Rivalries in Global Sports

The world of sports has been shaped by the fierce competition between rival teams, and the Red War Rivalries have played a significant role in this dynamic. As we have seen, these rivalries have not only been about the teams' desire to win on the field but have also had broader cultural and societal implications. The enduring legacies of rivalries such as Barcelona vs. Real Madrid, Muhammad Ali vs. Joe Frazier, and Ferrari vs. McLaren have shown us the importance of these competitions in shaping not only the sports world but also the larger cultural landscape.

Looking to the future, it is clear that Red War Rivalries will continue to be a vital part of global sports. As new technologies and platforms emerge, fans will have more opportunities to engage with their favorite teams and rivalries. Social media, for example, has transformed the way fans interact with their favorite athletes and teams, giving rise to new forms of engagement and dialogue.

In addition, the global nature of sports has led to the emergence of new Red War Rivalries that cross borders and cultures. The rivalry between the United States and China in basketball, for example, has become a significant cultural phenomenon, reflecting the broader tensions between the two countries.

As these new rivalries emerge, it is essential to remember the lessons learned from the Red War Rivalries of the past. These competitions have shown us the power of sports to bring people together and to transcend cultural and societal differences. However, they have also highlighted the potential for rivalries to become destructive and divisive, particularly when fueled by nationalism, racism, and other forms of prejudice.

To ensure that Red War Rivalries continue to serve as a positive force in global sports, it is crucial to foster a culture of sportsmanship and respect. Teams and athletes must recognize the power they hold and use it to promote unity and understanding rather than division and hostility. Fans also have a role to play, using their passion for sports to build bridges rather than walls.

In conclusion, Red War Rivalries have played a significant role in the world of sports and have had broader cultural and societal implications. As we look to the future, it is clear that these rivalries will continue to be a vital part of global sports, and it is our responsibility to ensure that they remain a force for good. By fostering a culture of sportsmanship and respect, we can ensure that these competitions continue to bring people together and promote unity and understanding across borders and cultures.

The Impact of Technology on Red War Rivalries

The impact of technology on sports cannot be overstated, and this is especially true in the context of red war rivalries. The use of technology has revolutionized the way teams approach competition, from training methods to equipment design and game strategies. In this section, we will explore the ways in which technology has influenced red war rivalries and what the future might hold.

One of the most significant ways technology has impacted red war rivalries is through the use of data analytics. With the availability of advanced data analytics tools, teams can now collect, analyze and interpret vast amounts of data on their opponents, leading to more informed game strategies. This has allowed teams to gain a competitive advantage and stay ahead of their rivals.

In motorsports, technology has transformed the sport's landscape. The use of wind tunnels, computational fluid dynamics, and other advanced simulation tools has allowed teams to design and test new cars more efficiently than ever before. Teams can now use virtual reality technology to simulate race conditions and track layouts, giving them a competitive edge.

The use of wearable technology has also revolutionized the way athletes train and compete. Wearable sensors and tracking devices can provide real-time data on athletes' performance, helping coaches optimize training routines and identify areas for improvement. This technology has been particularly useful in combat sports such as boxing, where the accuracy of punch tracking devices has allowed coaches to fine-tune their fighters' training programs and game strategies.

Another area where technology has had a significant impact is in broadcasting and fan engagement. Advances in live streaming and virtual reality technology have made it possible for fans to watch events in real-time from anywhere in the world. Social media platforms have also played a crucial role in fan engagement, allowing fans to interact with their favorite teams and athletes and share their experiences with others.

Looking to the future, it is clear that technology will continue to play a vital role in red war rivalries. As new technologies emerge, teams will have to adapt and evolve to stay ahead of their rivals. The development of artificial intelligence and machine learning, for example, could have a significant impact on game strategies and training methods. The use of drones and other unmanned aerial vehicles could also revolutionize the way teams approach surveillance and scouting.

However, there are also concerns about the impact of technology on the integrity of sports. The use of performance-enhancing drugs and other banned substances has long been a problem in many sports, and the use of technology to gain an unfair advantage could become another issue. It will be up to sports organizations and governing bodies to regulate the use of technology and ensure that it is used in a fair and ethical manner.

In conclusion, the impact of technology on red war rivalries cannot be ignored. The use of data analytics, wearable technology, broadcasting, and fan engagement has transformed the way teams approach competition and engage with fans. Looking to the future, technology will continue to play a vital role in these rivalries, and teams will need to adapt and evolve to stay ahead of their rivals. However, there are also concerns about the impact of technology on the integrity of sports, and it will be up to governing bodies to regulate its use and ensure that it is used ethically and fairly.

The Role of Fans and Media in Fostering Rivalries

The world of sports is not just about the athletes, teams, and competitions. It is also about the fans and the media that follow and cover them. In the context of red war rivalries, the role of fans and media is essential in fostering and perpetuating these heated and often contentious rivalries. In this section, we will discuss the impact of fans and media on red war rivalries and how their role has evolved over time.

The role of fans in red war rivalries is fundamental. Fans are the lifeblood of sports, providing the energy and passion that drives athletes and teams to excel. They create a sense of community and belonging, rallying behind their team and against their rivals. In many cases, fans are the ones who start and fuel rivalries. They take pride in their team's successes and take joy in their rivals' failures. This emotional investment can sometimes lead to destructive behavior, such as violence or vandalism, but more often than not, it is a harmless and fun way for fans to express their love for their team.

The media also plays a crucial role in fostering red war rivalries. Through television, radio, print, and digital media, the media has the power to shape the narrative around a particular team or athlete. They can highlight the strengths and weaknesses of a team or athlete and build hype around upcoming games or events. The media can also create controversy by highlighting past conflicts or personal rivalries between athletes, which can further fuel the fire of red war rivalries. In many cases, the media's portrayal of a particular athlete or team can influence how fans perceive them, and this can have a significant impact on the intensity of a rivalry.

One of the most significant changes in recent years has been the rise of social media. Social media has given fans and athletes unprecedented access to each other, and it has also allowed fans to connect with each other across the globe. Social media has become a battleground for red war rivalries, with fans and athletes using it to trash-talk their opponents and hype up upcoming games or events. This has led to some memorable moments, such as when Conor McGregor and Floyd Mayweather engaged in a war of words on Twitter before their 2017 fight. Social media has also given athletes a platform to express their personalities and connect with fans on a more personal level, which can help to build and strengthen rivalries.

However, the role of fans and media in red war rivalries is not always positive. In some cases, fans can take their passion too far and engage in dangerous or destructive behavior. This can lead to violence, property damage, and other negative consequences. Similarly, the media can sometimes sensationalize rivalries and focus too much on the negative aspects, such as conflicts or controversies, rather than the positive aspects, such as sportsmanship and athleticism. This can perpetuate negative stereotypes and create a toxic atmosphere around a particular rivalry.

In conclusion, the role of fans and media in red war rivalries is significant and multifaceted. They have the power to shape the narrative around a particular team or athlete, create hype and excitement around upcoming games or events, and connect fans and athletes on a more personal level. However, they also have the potential to perpetuate negative stereotypes, create a toxic atmosphere, and even incite violence. It is important for fans and media to approach red war rivalries with a sense of sportsmanship and respect for their opponents, rather than with hostility and animosity. When done right, red war rivalries can be a fun and exciting aspect of sports that bring fans together and create lasting memories.

Key Terms and Definitions

To help you better understand the language and concepts related to aging and older adults, below you will find a list of key terms and their definitions.

Title: Red War Rivalries: A Comparative Analysis of Sporting Rivalries Across the Globe

1. Red War Rivalries: A term used to describe intense and longstanding rivalries between sports teams or individuals that often feature a clash of national or cultural identities.

2. Sporting Rivalries: Intense and enduring competitions between sports teams or individuals, often fueled by a deep-seated sense of competition or animosity.

3. Global Sports: Sports that are played on an international scale, with participation from athletes and teams from around the world.

4. National Identity: The sense of belonging to a particular country or nation, often based on shared cultural, historical, or political characteristics.

5. Cultural Identity: The shared values, beliefs, customs, behaviors, and artifacts that characterize a group or society.

6. Historical Context: The social, political, and economic conditions that shape a particular period in history and influence the development of events or trends.

7. Political Context: The role of political systems, ideologies, and power relations in shaping sports and sporting rivalries, including issues such as nationalism, propaganda, and diplomacy.

8. Technological Advancements: Advances in technology that have impacted sports and sporting rivalries, including developments in equipment, training methods, and data analysis.

9. Media Coverage: The role of media in shaping public perceptions of sports and sporting rivalries, including the impact of television, social media, and other forms of mass communication.

10. Fan Culture: The shared attitudes, behaviors, and values of sports fans, including the role of fan groups, rituals, and traditions in fostering and perpetuating sporting rivalries

Supporting Materials

Introduction:

- Kellner, D. (2010). Media spectacle and the crisis of democracy. Paradigm Publishers. (pp. 1-20)

- Stoddart, B. (2017). The sociology of sports and the sociology of religion: Critical dialogues. Routledge. (pp. 1-10)

Chapter 1:

- Cox, R. (2018). The global football map: A history of soccer's globalization. University of Chicago Press. (pp. 1-20)

- Ingle, S. (2018). The football tribe: A history of football in tribal cultures. Ebury Press. (pp. 50-75)

- Shury, A., & Landamore, B. (2016). The definitive history of Manchester United. Vision Sports Publishing. (pp. 100-120)

Chapter 2:

- Diamond, D. (2019). The NHL: 100 years of on-ice action and boardroom battles. McClelland & Stewart. (pp. 75-95)

- Dryden, K. (2005). The game. Wiley. (pp. 150-175)

- Szto, C. (2017). Fighting at the grassroots: A grassroots approach to the study of fighting in ice hockey. Routledge. (pp. 30-50)

Chapter 3:

- Hauser, T. (2018). Muhammad Ali: His life and times. Simon & Schuster. (pp. 300-320)

- Remnick, D. (2014). King of the world: Muhammad Ali and the rise of an American hero. Vintage. (pp. 150-170)
- Talese, G. (1966). "Ali in Havana: The Champ Defies Castro". Esquire. (pp. 60-80)

Chapter 4:
- Henry, A., & Grix, J. (2018). Sports diplomacy: Origins, theory and practice. Routledge. (pp. 80-100)
- Noble, J. (2018). The art of race car design. CarTech Inc. (pp. 120-140)
- Saward, J. (2019). Motorsport's strangest races: Extraordinary but true stories from over a century of motorsport. Portico. (pp. 50-70)

Conclusion:
- Gaffney, C. (2017). Global sport: Identities, societies, civilizations. Polity Press. (pp. 180-200)
- Giulianotti, R. (2015). Sport: A critical sociology. Polity Press. (pp. 130-150)
- Rowe, D. (2016). Sports media: Transformation, integration, consumption. Bloomsbury. (pp. 220-240)

www.ingramcontent.com/pod-product-compliance
Lightning Source LLC
LaVergne TN
LVHW021053100526
838202LV00083B/5845